Wayne
Gretzky

Magician on the Ice

Aleksandrs Rozens

ROURKE ENTERPRISES,INC.
VERO BEACH, FLORIDA 32964

A Blackbirch Graphics book.

Library of Congress Cataloging-in-Publication Data

Rozens, Aleksandrs, 1967–
    Wayne Gretzky / by Aleksandrs Rozens.
        p.   cm. — (The winning spirit)
    Includes index.
    Summary: A biography of the star hockey player from Canada who has set many records while playing for the Edmonton Oilers and the Los Angeles Kings.
    ISBN 0-86592-119-9
    1. Gretzky, Wayne, 1961–   —Juvenile literature. 2. Hockey play-ers—Canada—Biography—Juvenile literature. [1. Gretzky, Wayne, 1961–   . 2. Hockey players.] I. Title.
GV848.5.G73R69   1993
796.962'092—dc20
[B]

MAR 9 – 1994   93-18132
                                                              CIP
                                                               AC

Contents

Starting Young
"The first one [Stanley Cup] is always the best."

*J*ust think how excited Wayne Gretzky and his young Canadian teammates on the Edmonton Oilers must have been. They had made it into the finals of the 1983–1984 Stanley Cup play-offs for the National Hockey League (NHL) title!

Wayne Gretzky and his teammates would have to face the defending-champion New York Islanders to win the cherished Stanley Cup. Wayne, though only 23 years old in that spring of 1984, was the team's captain. To top it all, the young Oilers had faced the Islanders in the previous Stanley Cup play-offs...and had lost.

The Islanders possessed enormous talent. The core of the team, center Bryan Trottier,

Opposite: Wayne Gretzky has dazzled spectators with his hockey talent since childhood. He was voted the National Hockey League's Most Valuable Player for every year during the 1980s except one.

wing Mike Bossy, and defenseman Denis Potvin had been on six Stanley Cup championship teams and had won four Stanley Cups in a row. The upstart Oilers team had been in the National Hockey League just a few years. "Drive for five!" cheered Islanders fans, confident their team would be the first ever to win five Stanley Cups in a row.

The Islanders were older and somewhat more experienced, but Wayne and the Oilers prided themselves on being quicker on their skates. Moreover, they were as confident as the Islanders and just as eager to win. They had come close to winning the year before, but this time they felt they could finally take the Stanley Cup home.

The Stanley Cup finals, a seven-game series, did not start well for Wayne and his teammates. Even though they won the first game 1-0, they did not play well. In the second game they were beaten 6-1. But the young Oilers didn't give up. They rallied to win the next two games, setting themselves up with an opportunity to win a fourth game, and the Stanley Cup. As the captain of the team, Wayne never let his teammates get discouraged. Just imagine how nervous the Oilers must have felt in their fifth game as they played in front of their hometown fans in Edmonton and huge television audiences across Canada and the United States.

"I've won a lot of awards in my life," Wayne told his teammates before they went on to the ice to play that fifth game. "I've had a lot of personal success, but nothing I've done means more than this."

Wayne's dreams came true. The Oilers won that fifth game, 5-2, and, for Wayne, that first Stanley Cup victory will always be special. "The first one is always the best," he said.

But Wayne's road to Stanley Cup victory was a long, hard one. Before that game, Wayne had spent a lifetime practicing and training.

On Skates at Two

Wayne Gretzky was born on January 26, 1961. He grew up in Brantford, Canada, which is not far from the cities of Toronto, in Canada, and Detroit, in the United States.

Wayne's grandmother, Mary Gretzky, was an immigrant from Poland. His grandfather was from Russia. Together they started a big vegetable farm in Brantford.

Wayne's father, Walter, worked for Bell Telephone as a repairman. After he suffered a job-related accident, Walter was plagued by a constant hearing problem.

Wayne had three brothers, Glen, Keith, and Brent, as well as a sister, Kim. Walter Gretzky and Wayne's mother, Phyllis, were not rich, but they sacrificed a lot and worked hard to buy Wayne new hockey sticks and skates.

Wayne was two years old when he learned how to skate. You may think this is an early age to start, but in Canada hockey is a very popular sport, just as baseball is in the United States. In Canada, even the smallest of towns has its own hockey rink for young players. These rinks are not as modern as those used by professional teams, but they are the perfect places for players to practice and learn.

Wayne's First Coach

Walter Gretzky drove his son to his first hockey practices in a blue station wagon that the family named "The Blue Goose."

Wayne practiced his shooting for long hours. He would even take shots against the foundation of the family's house. Whenever Walter would go outside to ask Wayne to stop practicing against the wall, only a few minutes would go by before young Wayne would start up all over again. "He practically caved it in," remembers the proud father.

The Gretzky family shared Wayne's love for hockey and athletics. His brothers, Keith, Glen, and Brent, also played hockey. Glen's competitive spirit might have been even greater than his famous older brother's, but Glen was born with club feet, which made skating painful. Wayne's sister was a track star, whose career was cut short by an injury. The entire Gretzky family, including Wayne's grandmother, would

Wayne's family was the first to foster the young athlete's interest in hockey. His grandmother often took her turn playing goalie in the living room.

often watch a popular Canadian television show called *Hockey Night In Canada*. Sometimes Wayne's grandmother would even play goalie, or goaltender, for Wayne when he practiced with a rubber ball.

When Wayne was four years old, his father took a lawn sprinkler and turned the family's backyard into a hockey rink. One can only imagine what the hardware-store owner must have been thinking when Wayne's mother went to buy a lawn sprinkler in the middle of winter. But, from inside his warm home, Walter Gretzky could keep an eye on Wayne without

Because their son was such a natural hockey player, the Gretzkys decided to build a homemade rink in their backyard. When he wasn't in school, Wayne was usually on the rink practicing.

having to stand outside in the cold. All he had to do was peek outside a window.

Wayne would even practice before school, from seven to eight-thirty in the morning. When he came home at three-thirty in the afternoon, he would practice until dinner. He would play again after dinner until nine. On weekends he would play in games with other young Brantford hockey players.

Weekend evenings were just for Wayne and his father, who would coach him. Wayne would practice shooting and handling the hockey puck with his stick by skating in and around empty detergent bottles. This type of training helped Wayne develop a good skating stride and the ability to make sharp turns. His father thought Wayne could also use the old detergent bottles as targets to strengthen his forehand and backhand shots.

Sometimes Walter would invite older boys in the neighborhood to play with Wayne. This helped Wayne build up his skills and overcome any fear of playing against bigger guys. It was an experience that would prove valuable in the coming years. In the future, when Wayne was all grown up and a professional star, he would almost always be the smallest player on the ice.

2

Early Victories

"Wayne...one day you're gonna have so many trophies, we're not gonna have room for them all."

*I*n Canada, hockey players up to the age of 11 can play in the Atom League. Wayne started playing in the Brantford Atom League when he was six and began competing against much bigger boys.

In the Brantford Atom League, Wayne's sweater was so large on him that it got in the way of his shooting. His father showed him how to tuck the sweater into his pants on his shooting side. Even today, Wayne continues to do this.

In his first year with the Brantford Atom League, Wayne scored only one goal. When Walter found out that Wayne was disappointed about not winning a trophy, he told his son, "Wayne, keep practicing, and one day you're gonna have so many trophies, we're not gonna have room for them all."

Wayne took his father's advice. And even though he enjoyed many other sports, like baseball and lacrosse, Wayne continued to practice hockey day and night.

Setting an Unbroken Record

The work paid off. The next year, Wayne scored 27 goals for his team. The year after that, he scored 104. And three years after that one-goal-no-trophy season, Wayne scored 196 goals. By the time Wayne was 10, he had scored 378 goals in 69 games! He had broken the league record by an amazing 238 points! To this day, that record has not been broken.

Wayne has spent most of his career competing with players much bigger than he. At age 6, he often skated against 11-year-olds in Canada's Atom League.

Although, as a young boy, Wayne was equally good at lacrosse and hockey, he decided that he would concentrate his efforts in the rink.

Wayne's talent was quickly recognized. At the young age of 10, Wayne was being interviewed by reporters. One of the newspaper writers nicknamed him "The Great Gretzky." It was a nickname that would stick. Wayne even had fans asking him for his autograph. It got so

bad that sometimes Wayne would disguise
himself by wearing goalie Greg Stefan's team
jacket. That trick worked, but when Greg
posed as Wayne and signed autographs, he
would always misspell Wayne's last name
without realizing it, writing an *s* instead of a *z*.

Popularity Brings Jealousy

Being the most popular player on his team was
not always that much fun.

Some of the parents of Wayne's teammates
accused him of being a puck hog. They would
come to games with a stopwatch to see how
long Wayne would keep the puck.

But Wayne's stats seem to show a player
willing to share the glory. In one year—in
79 games—he had 120 assists. To this day, in
professional hockey, Wayne prides himself on
passing more to teammates than taking shots
for himself.

If Wayne's team lost a game, some of the
other players' parents would blame him for the
loss. While Wayne's family supported him,
some people criticized him. They said his
record-breaking streak would not last.

The criticism got so bad that Wayne's mom
stopped going to the games. Many of the
people who criticized Wayne's playing were
simply jealous. Wayne's dad, however, continued to go to Wayne's games to cheer for him.
He paid little attention to what others said.

Young Wayne Meets His Hero

When he was 11, Wayne met his hockey hero, the great Gordie Howe. Howe had played with the Detroit Red Wings and had set the National Hockey League's record for points scored in a career. For young Wayne this was a truly great moment. When Howe asked Wayne if he was keeping up with his practicing, Wayne nervously answered yes.

At age 11, Wayne met his hockey hero, Gordie Howe. To this day, Wayne still believes that Howe was "the best player who ever played hockey and the best man who ever played in sports."

"But, do you practice your backhand?"
Howe asked.

"Yes, sir, I do," said Wayne.

"Good. Make sure you keep practicing that backhand," Howe advised him.

It seems fairly certain that Wayne took Gordie Howe's advice to heart because most of the records he would set as a professional would be with his backhand. In fact, the Gretzky backhand became a shot that NHL goalies learned to respect and fear.

Away from Home

At 13, Wayne had his own agent representing him. Known throughout Canada, he traveled across the country to play in games that were always packed with fans who came to see "The Great Gretzky."

When Wayne was 14, a friend invited him to Toronto to play hockey. There was a team in Toronto that Wayne could play with, and his friend offered to let Wayne stay with his family.

At first, Wayne's parents would not let him go to Toronto. They were worried about their son being on his own in a big city. Toronto was very different from small-town Brantford and could even be dangerous for young people. But Wayne convinced his parents to let him go.

For Wayne it was a big victory. He'd be able to play for Toronto's top bantam league.

It was also the perfect opportunity to get away from all those jealous parents that kept wishing Wayne would fail.

When Wayne tried out for Toronto's bantam team, the coaches thought he played so well that they had him try out for a Junior B team, which had 20-year-old players. At only 135 pounds, Wayne was once again one of the smallest players. His size, however, didn't stop him from scoring two goals in his first game with the Toronto Young Nationals. The two goals proved to the young and small Wayne that he'd actually be "all right" in his tough new league.

The practices that Walter Gretzky had arranged for his son against older players in their backyard "rink" had paid off.

But those days in Toronto were also difficult for Wayne. He was lonely. Although he could call his family during the week, he could visit them only on weekends. He was homesick for an entire year, often asking himself if he had made a big mistake by coming.

3

Scoring His Way to Edmonton

In his first year with the Greyhounds, Wayne broke the all-time Junior A scoring record.

*W*hen he was just 16, Wayne Gretzky was asked to play for the Sault Ste. Marie Greyhounds. This was indeed something to be proud of because the Greyhounds were a Junior A team. The Junior A level was the top level for amateur hockey players who were under 20 years of age.

At first, Wayne didn't want to play with Sault Ste. Marie because it meant spending more time away from home. His father even wrote a letter to the Greyhounds, asking them not to pick his son for the team.

There was nothing for Wayne and his dad to do but go to Sault Ste. Marie to try to explain why Wayne didn't want to play for the Junior A Greyhounds.

Wayne Joins the Greyhounds

The Gretzkys' pleas were ignored. The Greyhounds wanted Wayne, and they wouldn't take no for an answer. Eventually, Wayne got to like the Greyhounds and Angelo Bumbacco, who ran the team. He decided to stay. His contract with the team was very fair. In it, the team agreed to pay for Wayne's college if he didn't stay with the team or if he got injured.

Sault Ste. Marie was far from Brantford, so Wayne stayed with an old friend named Steve Bodnar. Steve and Wayne had played in the Brantford Peewee League together.

The team looked after Wayne. When Mr. Bumbacco saw that Wayne needed a new coat, he took him to a store and bought him one.

Wayne started wearing the number 99 on his team sweater when he was playing with the Greyhounds. His favorite player, Gordie Howe, wore number 9. Wayne wanted to wear number 9, too, but it was already being worn by one of the Greyhounds. Wayne decided to wear number 99. In his first game, number 99, scored three goals and made three assists. To this day, Wayne wears number 99.

Wayne earned 25 dollars a week with the Greyhounds. He was still one of the smaller players on the team, and in the team's early practices he didn't always play well. At Sault Ste. Marie, Wayne had little free time. With all the practicing to be done with the team, plus

When he was 16, Wayne was invited to play for the Sault Ste. Marie Greyhounds, a top-level amateur team in Canada. The team's manager, Angelo Bumbacco, looked out for the young hockey star who was far from home.

his homework, there was little time for much else that was any fun. Although he didn't know it at the time, 16-year-old Wayne had left home, and his childhood, for good.

The Greyhounds would travel to games in other cities, and Wayne wouldn't get back until early in the morning. His hockey responsibilities became so great that Wayne never got his high school diploma. Later, he was offered a high school diploma for 35 dollars, but he turned it down. He felt that getting a diploma without working for it wasn't right.

During his first year with the Greyhounds, Wayne broke the all-time Junior A scoring record. His Greyhound fans nicknamed him "Pretzel" because he skated hunched over.

Turning Pro

Soon after the Greyhounds' coach, Muzz MacPherson, left the team, Wayne started to look for another club. "Without Muzz, 'The Soo' [Sault Ste. Marie] suddenly felt a lot colder," Wayne remembers. He was too young to play on a National Hockey League team, but he could play in the World Hockey Association, a new league competing with the NHL. Wayne Gretzky, age 17, was about to become a professional athlete.

Wayne was offered several contracts from Canadian and U.S. teams that played in the World Hockey Association league. One person who was interested in hiring Wayne was a man from Vancouver named Nelson Skalbania.

Nelson Skalbania interviewed Wayne while they were jogging one day. Skalbania, a dedicated jogger, wanted to see just how good an athlete Wayne was. Together they ran seven miles. On the last mile there was a steep hill. Wayne sprinted as fast as he could up that hill and, at the top, he tried not to show how tired he was. He must have impressed Nelson Skalbania, who quickly signed Wayne Gretzky to his team, the Indianapolis Racers.

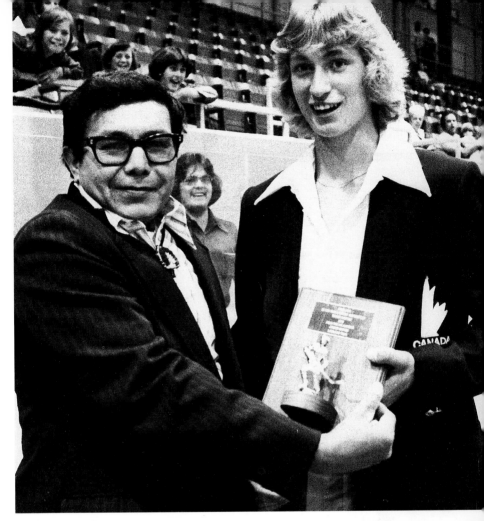

Wayne attended a special ceremony in 1978 to celebrate his signing with the Indianapolis Racers.

But things did not work out as planned. In his eight games with the Indianapolis Racers, Wayne didn't play very well. Mr. Skalbania decided to move Wayne to another team, but he allowed Wayne to pick the team that he would eventually be transferred to.

With the help of his agent, Wayne chose the Edmonton Oilers. It was a choice that would make history.

4

Skating to the Top

**"I won it [Stanley Cup] for my mom
and my dad and the rest of my
family and for me, too."**

*E*dmonton is the capital of Alberta, one of
Canada's 10 provinces. It is located on the
North Saskatchewan River and is a trade center
for farmers in western Canada. Many oil com-
panies supply nearby oil fields and coalfields
with materials from Edmonton.

In their early days, the Edmonton Oilers
were well respected in the World Hockey
Association and were expected to make it into
the National Hockey League. If the Oilers
became part of the NHL, it would mean more
people at the games and more profits for the
team owners.

The Edmonton Oilers' owner, Peter
Pocklington, signed Wayne Gretzky without
ever having seen him play. He had apparently

heard about Wayne's talent. Wayne was given a 10-year, 3-million-dollar contract with the Edmonton Oilers. The day he signed was his eighteenth birthday. Once again, Wayne, who played center, was the youngest and smallest member of his team.

Wayne's roommate in Edmonton was Ace Bailey. One of the very first things Ace taught Wayne about life in Edmonton was to keep two sets of car keys. The first set of keys was for Wayne to carry around. The second was for Wayne's car ignition, to keep the engine running. Why? Winters are so cold in Edmonton that once you turn your car off, you may not be able to get it running again.

In his first year with the Edmonton Oilers (1978–1979), Wayne was named Rookie of the Year. By 1983, he was captain of the team.

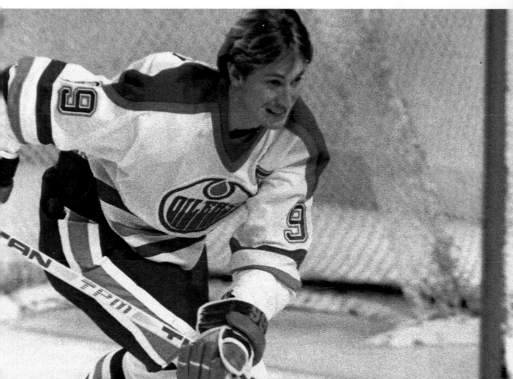

Rookie of the Year

Wayne liked playing in the World Hockey Association league. The games were faster, and the players didn't check (bump) one another as much as they did in junior hockey leagues. Wayne, who weighed only 155 pounds, was still undersized. One tough check from a far bigger player could end his hockey career.

The team's coach, Glen Sather, took care of Wayne. Mrs. Sather cooked meals for Wayne when he first arrived in Edmonton. Sather predicted that one day the Oilers would be part of the National Hockey League and that Wayne would be its captain.

Wayne's first season with the Edmonton Oilers was a big success. The team made it into the World Hockey League play-offs, and Wayne was named Rookie of the Year. In that glorious 1978–1979 season, Wayne scored 43 goals and 104 points. He had become a star.

Wayne's First NHL Season

The first of Coach Sather's predictions came true the next season—the Edmonton Oilers made it to the National Hockey League.

For the 1979–1980 season, the Oilers got two very important players from other teams. One of them was Kevin Lowe, who played defense. The other was Mark Messier, who played center. Both players became good friends with Wayne. All three became stars.

The Oilers lost their first National Hockey League game. Wayne didn't score a goal until the fifth game. His first NHL season was difficult for him—he had developed tonsillitis, but he didn't want to miss a game. Slowly, Wayne began to pick up speed, and he began to score. Even in that slow-starting season Wayne scored 50 goals, and he was only 19! Wayne was the youngest player in the history of the NHL to score that many goals.

Although he didn't win the Art Ross Trophy for the league's leading scorer, Wayne did win the Lady Byng Trophy for good sportsmanship. For Wayne, the Lady Byng Trophy was more important because it showed the world that Walter and Phyllis Gretzky had taught their son how important fair play really is.

That 1979–80 season, Wayne and the Edmonton Oilers got into the Stanley Cup playoffs but lost against the powerful Philadelphia Flyers. Despite the Oilers' loss, NHL players and fans agreed it was a pretty good start for such a young team.

Breaking an NHL Record

The 1980–1981 season was a breakthrough for Wayne and the Oilers. Wayne broke the league's single-season-assist record and the single-season-points total. Since he enjoyed setting up goals for other players, Wayne was excited about the new honor he received. He got just as much of a thrill when he assisted in a score as when he scored himself. The thrill was in seeing a team work together. One can only wonder what some of those parents who had accused Wayne of being a puck hog might have been thinking after Wayne proved to the fans that he certainly was a "team" player.

Trying for the Stanley Cup

In the 1980–1981 Stanley Cup play-offs, the Edmonton Oilers played the Montreal Canadiens in the semifinals. The Montreal Canadiens were a feared and respected team. In its history, the team had won 21 Stanley Cups. But, most important, the Canadiens had won the Stanley Cup four times in a row. Wayne and the Oilers were clearly nervous. Even Coach Sather didn't think his team could win. Before the games, he told his players that even if they didn't win against the Canadiens, they would still gain a lot from the experience of playing such a strong team.

The Oilers surprised everybody, including themselves, when they won three games in a row against the Montreal Canadiens and took the semifinals. They would face the defending Stanley Cup champions, the New York Islanders, in the final Stanley Cup games.

The finals were a letdown. The team's hopes had started out sky-high, but they ended up shattered. The Oilers lost to the Islanders

Wayne makes his way toward the net during a 1983 play-off game against the Black Hawks. Although the Oilers played well that season, they eventually lost the Stanley Cup to the New York Islanders.

four games to two. Once again, the young team had gained lots of attention and earned more respect. But it wasn't enough. Wayne and the Oilers wanted a taste of victory. They were ready, or so they believed.

More Losses

Later in 1981, Wayne played on Canada's national team. This team played hockey clubs representing other countries for the famous Canadian Cup.

The training for the Canadian national team was brutal. There were two hours of practice in the morning and two hours of practice in the afternoon. The Canadians did well in the Cup semifinals, defeating the United States, but their toughest match was against the Soviet Union.

The Winning Spirit

There was a great rivalry between both teams because both countries took great pride in their hockey teams. Some Canadian hockey fans even believed that hockey was a sport that only Canadians could play well. The dominant Soviet hockey team, the reigning world champions, changed this type of thinking. In fact, many Soviet players were later courted by the National Hockey League.

The Canadian team lost against the Soviet team with a score of 8-1. It was a tough game. The Soviet goaltender, Vladislav Tretiak, just would not let any shots get by him, including Wayne's. For Wayne, the experience was both positive and negative. He had lost an important championship series for the second time in months, but he had also gained invaluable exposure to some of the world's greatest players.

In the 1981–82 season, the Edmonton team drafted Grant Fuhr, the first black goaltender in the NHL. Liked and respected by his teammates, Fuhr was also a fiercely competitive athlete. In close games, Fuhr's ability to make game-saving stops was amazing.

That season, Wayne set an NHL scoring record by reaching the 50-goal mark in only 39 games. Halfway through the season, Wayne reached a mark that only a handful of players had ever achieved during a regular season. By his 66th game, Wayne had scored 77 goals, a record achieved only by Phil Esposito, a man who had played for the Chicago Black Hawks, the Boston Bruins, and the New York Rangers. It took Esposito 70 games to score the same number of points. Everybody who saw Wayne score his 77th goal cheered for him. Even President Ronald Reagan called afterward with congratulations.

That year, Wayne and the Edmonton Oilers failed to win the Stanley Cup play-offs. They lost against the Los Angeles Kings, a team most experts agreed was not as good as the Oilers.

In the 1982–1983 season, Wayne was given the *Sports Illustrated* Sportsman of the Year Award for both his hockey skills and his sportsmanship. Wayne had often spoken out against all the fighting that went on among hockey players, which he saw as something that made many people turn away from the sport.

In that same season, Wayne broke his own single-season-assist record. He won his fourth Hart Trophy, but, once again, his team was stopped by the New York Islanders in the Stanley Cup play-offs. The Oilers won the first game against the Islanders, but the Islanders came back to earn their fourth consecutive Stanley Cup victory.

Many hockey fans and newspaper sportswriters began to wonder if Wayne could take the pressures of playing in a final Stanley Cup game. The Oilers had come so close to winning so many times. Sure, Wayne was a great

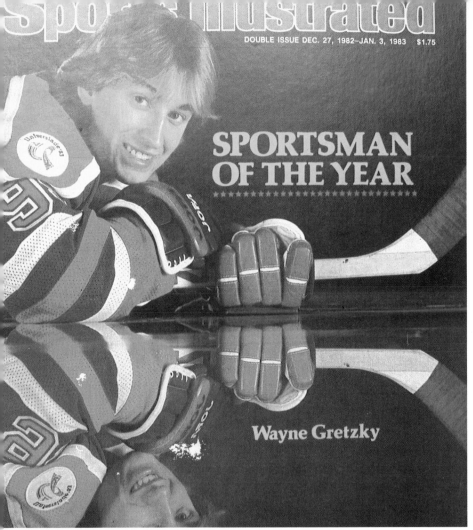

SPORTSMAN
OF THE YEAR
★★★★★★★★★★★★★★★★★★★★★★★★★★★★★★★★★

Wayne Gretzky

In 1983, Wayne was named Sportsman of the Year by Sports Illustrated magazine. He is known throughout the sports world for his good nature and talent.

player during the regular season games, they said, but he never seemed to be able to win in the finals. Wayne had broken so many scoring and assist records, but could he and the Oilers ever win a Stanley Cup?

When Wayne passed the New York Islanders' locker room after the Islanders' Stanley Cup victory, he saw something that many fans never

**The
Winning
Spirit**

get to see. Inside the hot, sweat-filled Islanders
locker room, players were putting ice on their
knees and rubbing sore shoulders. Some had
black eyes, and some had bloody mouths.
Wayne remarked that it looked more like a
morgue than a champion's locker room. Kevin
Lowe, his friend and teammate who also saw
the locker room, said, "That's how you win
championships."

Both realized that the Oilers would have to
play the final games the way they played regular season games. If the Oilers could get to the
championships that next season, they would
have to fight for every victory until the very last
second of the last game of the Stanley Cup
finals. And that's exactly what the Edmonton
Oilers did the following season.

Wayne Becomes the Oilers' Captain

The 1983–84 season was a difficult one. But it
was also the season Coach Sather's second
prediction came true—Wayne was made captain of the Oilers. As the team fought to get
back into the Stanley Cup championship finals,
people were once again wondering if Wayne
and his teammates could win "the big one."
They were up against their old rivals, the New
York Islanders, who were hoping to be the first
NHL team to win five Stanley Cups in a row.
No one had ever done that, not even the great
Montreal Canadiens.

Four Stanley Cups

The Oilers surprised the Islanders in New York by winning the first game, but the Islanders won game two. During that game, Islanders fans were singing the theme to the Mickey Mouse Club: "Who's the leader of Jamboree? M-I-C-K-E-Y M-O-U-S-E." Why that song? Islanders fans had a joke that went like this: "What do Mickey Mouse and Wayne Gretzky have in common? Neither has scored against the Islanders in the Stanley Cup play-offs."

The situation was almost as bad as when parents at the Brantford Atom League games would sit on the side of the rink with stop-watches, trying to time just how long Wayne held the puck.

The Oilers managed to hold on, and the play-offs continued in Edmonton. There, the Oilers would have their own fans for support. And, a win could be well celebrated.

The next three games were tough. In game three, the Oilers won by five goals, 7-2. But, again, Wayne didn't score a goal.

The Islanders' defensemen were keeping a close eye on Wayne. He may not have scored against them in other finals, but they were not going to take any chances. They stayed with Wayne even after he had passed the puck. That way, there was less chance of the puck being passed back for a shot on goal. To beat their strategy, Wayne decided to wait an extra moment before he passed the puck—spoiling the Islanders' timing and giving himself an extra second to receive a return pass.

In game four, Wayne's defense worked, and he scored two goals. The Islanders' jinx on him was broken, and Islanders fans stopped singing about Mickey Mouse.

The Oilers then won the fifth and last game against the mighty Islanders and celebrated their first Stanley Cup victory.

They passed the large trophy cup around to one another. Some kissed it, and some drank champagne from it.

The Edmonton Oilers had been a part of the National Hockey League for only five years when they won the Stanley Cup. For Wayne and his teammates it was the first of four Stanley Cup victories that would follow in the coming years. Wayne remembers the victory against the Islanders as his favorite because it was the first.

About the Stanley Cup, Wayne says fondly: "For me, it made everything I'd done, worked at, or been through all worthwhile: all the practice and pylons, all the critics and the loneliness, all the headlines and the doubters. I won it for my dad and my mom and the rest of my family and for me, too."

The next year, in the 1985 season, Wayne and the Oilers won the Stanley Cup against the Philadelphia Flyers.

In the 1986 season, the Oilers didn't make it to the Stanley Cup finals. The Oilers started out well. They were the best in the league, but the Calgary Flames won against them in the play-off games.

Wayne and the Edmonton Oilers came back in the 1987 season to win their third Stanley Cup. Again their victims were the Philadelphia Flyers.

It seemed that Wayne and the Oilers were unstoppable. With Wayne on the ice, goaltenders had lots to worry about. "There are only so many options a player has when he has

Wayne and Oilers teammate Mark Messier hold up the Stanley Cup trophy after their 6-3 win over the Boston Bruins in 1988. It was the Oilers' fourth Stanley Cup victory.

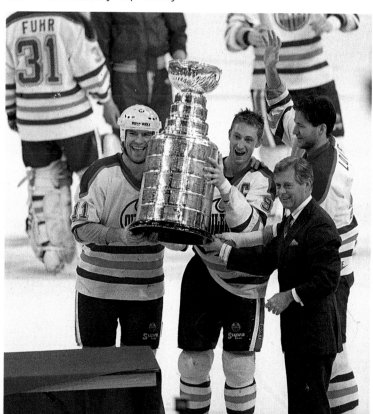

the puck, but it seems like Wayne always has two or three more," said New York Rangers goalie Mike Richter, who called Wayne "the best hockey player ever."

In 1987, Wayne also played on the NHL's all-star team against the Soviet Union. Even though the match ended up as a split decision, Wayne was voted the team's most valuable player. Wayne's skillful playing and his good sportsmanship earned him the respect and admiration of the Soviet team.

In 1988, Wayne and his teammates won their fourth Stanley Cup. This time their victory was against the Boston Bruins.

A "Royal" Wedding and a Shock

Later in 1988—in July—Wayne married an American actress named Janet Jones. Janet was from St. Louis, Missouri, but had moved to Los Angeles, California, to work. She is known for her roles in the movies *The Flamingo Kid* and *A Chorus Line*. Wayne and Janet had met in 1981, but they didn't start seeing each other on a regular basis until 1987.

Wayne and Janet's wedding was held in Edmonton. Wayne's teammates—old and new—came to the wedding. His hero, Gordie Howe, with whom he had become friends, was also there. The news of Wayne and Janet's wedding even reached the Soviet Union. Goalkeeper Vladislav Tretiak, a former rival and

Wayne and American actress Janet Jones were married in 1988 in Edmonton. Because Wayne is considered such a hero in Canada, newspapers compared the couple's ceremony with a royal wedding.

now a friend, traveled 6,000 miles to attend the wedding. In Canada, where there are no kings or queens, newspapers called Wayne and Janet's wedding "royal." After all, Wayne was the king of hockey.

But for Canada the excitement would not last. In August of 1988, Edmonton Oilers fans heard news that surprised and saddened them. Wayne's teammates were as surprised as his fans. Wayne Gretzky, the best hockey player of his time, perhaps of any time, would no longer play with the Edmonton Oilers. He had been traded to the Los Angeles Kings.

An era was over.

5

New Beginnings

"The thought of not being able to play was really frightening."

*T*he news that Wayne Gretzky had been traded to the Los Angeles Kings shocked both Edmonton Oilers fans and hockey fans across Canada and the United States. After nine seasons with the Oilers and four Stanley Cups, the glorious Gretzky era was over. Wayne would be playing with the Los Angeles Kings. His new team was not a bad team, but it certainly wasn't the best in the NHL. Wayne saw the change as a challenge. He would see if he could help make the Kings a winning team.

A Teary Farewell

Joining the Los Angeles Kings was difficult for Wayne. After playing with the Oilers for his entire career in the National Hockey League,

In August of 1988, Wayne announced that he was leaving the Oilers for the Los Angeles Kings. Although he viewed the move as a challenge, Wayne was deeply saddened to leave his family and his homeland of Canada.

he had made many close friends, and the team had become a family. As Wayne made public that he had agreed to be traded, he began to cry. It filled him with such emotion that he could not finish his statement to the press.

Some fans wanted to blame Wayne's wife for the trade. They said that she wanted to break up Wayne and the Oilers. Wayne was so popular with his Canadian fans—and they were so attached to him—that headlines and stories about the trade in the newspapers made Wayne's decision sound like a major blow to the country. "Canada Loses National Treasure," one newspaper wrote. Another newspaper reporter, who lived in Edmonton, even wrote that Wayne "was the best reason for living here." Some Edmonton fans blamed the team's owner, Peter Pocklington, who traded Wayne and two of his teammates to the Kings for more than 10 million dollars.

In Los Angeles, where hockey is strictly an indoor sport, the Gretzky-led Kings became instantly popular. Suddenly people by the thousands were buying season tickets. Kings owner Bruce McNall and Wayne became good friends. Bruce tried to do his best to make Wayne feel comfortable.

Wayne found a home in Encino, near Los Angeles, where he and Janet are raising their two children. One of the many things Wayne likes about Los Angeles is that he can ride around in his car with the top down.

With Wayne gone, the Edmonton Oilers are still a good team, but they have lost a special ingredient that was important to their morale. Wayne's old fans, however, are not bitter. In his first game against the Oilers in Edmonton, he got a standing ovation from the Edmonton crowd. In 1989, Wayne broke Gordie Howe's NHL record for career points when he scored career point number 1,851. What was interesting about this record-breaking event was that Wayne achieved it with a backhand shot—the very shot that Howe had told the young Wayne to practice!

Although Wayne broke Howe's record, he still says that his hockey hero is "the best player who ever played hockey and the best man who ever played sports."

Wayne gets a hug of congratulations from his idol, hockey legend Gordie Howe, after he broke Howe's scoring record of 1,850 points on October 15, 1989.

Playing Against Friends

In the 1991–1992 season Wayne and the Kings finished in first place. What must have been really strange for Wayne was that the Kings had to play the Edmonton Oilers in the division finals. The team that won those games got to play in the Stanley Cup finals.

"This was tricky," Wayne recalled. "I wanted like crazy to win that series, but at the same time, I didn't want my buddies, the Stanley Cup defending champions, to lose. I never enjoyed a minute of it."

What may have been the most difficult part of those play-off games was that during those division finals Wayne and his old teammates never spoke to each other. The battle for the division finals was a close one between the Kings and the Oilers, but the Oilers won.

A Second Chance

Unfortunately, a serious back injury kept Wayne off the ice during the first part of the 1992–1993 season. In fact, the injury threatened to cut short his career.

For five months, Wayne had to be careful not to strain his back. On airplane trips he had to get special permission to lie on the floor. There were some funny moments during this difficult period for Wayne, such as the time when he stretched out flat on his back in a restaurant and a waitress thought that he had had a little too much to drink.

Although "The Great Gretzky" was not skating with them early in the year, the Kings started off their 1992–1993 season with a 19-7-2 record in their first 28 games. But Wayne's fans and his teammates missed him.

For a while, it looked as if Wayne would have to undergo a serious operation involving his spinal cord. Fortunately it turned out that he did not need the operation. However, he did have to take extra care of his back, which meant staying off the ice and resting. "I figured that would be it for me because all I was told by the doctors is if you have any kind of pain, you can't play. I thought my career was over," said Wayne.

Wayne even joked that he had started to look at other careers—he once hinted at coaching first base for the Toronto Blue Jays.

Wayne was recovering, and he didn't have to leave the hockey rink for the baseball diamond. On January 4, 1993, Wayne and his doctors announced that he would soon return to the ice. He would lace up his skates for a game against the Tampa Bay Lightning. For Wayne, this was a great moment. "I'm fortunate to be getting a second chance. I worked hard to get this second chance. It's something I really wanted," he said that day.

But this game was special for another reason, too. It was "The Great Gretzky's" 1,000th NHL career game.

Wayne was supported and encouraged by the loyal fans. The game was sold out, and there were celebrities in the crowd who had come to see Wayne Gretzky's return. He even got a standing ovation from fans, who were waving "Welcome Back Wayne" signs.

The actual game against the Tampa Bay Lightning, however, was not so simple.

For the most part, players from the Tampa Bay Lightning were nervous about accidently hurting Wayne. After all, nobody wanted to be remembered as the player who cut short "The Great Gretzky's" return. When Tampa Bay's defenseman Peter Taglianetti bumped into Wayne, he grabbed him just to make sure he would not fall—good sportsmanship not often seen in hockey. But Wayne did not need anybody's help that night. He was fast on the

In January 1993, Wayne announced his return to professional hockey. After months of training and therapy, his doctors gave him permission to return to the game.

ice, knowing just where the puck would end up and beating his opponents to it. Although the Kings lost, Wayne had two assists. This was an impressive contribution for someone just back in the game after such a serious injury.

When his days on the ice are truly over, it will probably be said that Wayne Gretzky was the greatest hockey player ever to lace up a pair of skates. More important, it will also probably be said that he was one of the best-loved and most-admired players in the game. Not bad for a kid from Brantford!

Glossary

assist The action of a hockey player who, by passing a puck, enables a teammate to make a goal.

backhand A shot made with the back of the hand turned in the direction of movement of the puck.

center The hockey player whose position is in the middle area facing the center of the rink.

puck The rubber disk that hockey players hit with their sticks to score a goal.

rival One who competes against another.

rookie A first-year participant in a professional sport.

Stanley Cup The trophy awarded each year to the National Hockey League champions.

For Further Reading

Aaseng, Nathan. *Hockey's Super Scorers.* Minneapolis, MN: Lerner Publications, 1984.

Ericson, Marc. *Hockey Superstars.* Chicago: Kidsbooks, 1991.

Leder, Jane M. *Wayne Gretzky.* New York: Crestwood House, 1985.

Raber, Tom. *Wayne Gretzky: Hockey Great.* Minneapolis, MN: Lerner Publications, 1991.

Ward, Carl. *Hockey.* New York: Sterling, 1991.

Index

Photo Credits:
Cover: Wide World Photos; p. 4: Wide World Photos; p. 14: ©Howard Liuick/The Expositor; p. 16: ©Jack Bowman/The Expositor; p. 23: ©Frank Burt/The Expositor; pp. 25, 29, 32, 36, 38, 40, 42, 45: Wide World Photos.

Illustrations by Charles Shaw.